# LONG CIR(

# WALKS

# IN

# NOTTINGHAMSHIRE

*Happy walking!*
*John N. Merrill*

## by

# JOHN N. MERRILL

Maps and photographs by John N. Merrill

## TRAIL CREST PUBLICATIONS Ltd.,

*- "from footprint to finished book."*

# 1994

Sandia Mountains
New Mexico. USA

# TRAIL CREST
# PUBLICATIONS
# Ltd.,

**Milne House
Speedwell Mill,
Miller's Green,
Wirksworth,
Derbyshire
DE4 4BL**

**(0629) 826354
(0629) 826354**

Edited, typeset, designed, paged, printed, marketed and distributed by John N. Merrill.

© Text, walks, Maps, & photographs
John N. Merrill/Suncrest Ventures Ltd. 1994.

First Published - June 1994

ISBN 1 874754 22 5

*U.S.A.
office -
P.O. Box 124,
Santa Rosa,
New Mexico
88435
U.S.A.*

**Please note** - The maps in this guide are purely illustrative. You are encouraged to use the appropriate 1:25,000 O.S. map.

Meticulous research has been undertaken to ensure that this publication is highly accurate at the time of going to press. The publishers, however, cannot be held responsible for alterations, errors or omissions, but they would welcome notification of such for future editions.

Typeset in - Bookman - bold, italic and plain 9pt and 18pt.

Printed by - Footprint Press Ltd./John N. Merrill at Milne House, Speedwell Mill, Miller's Green, Wirksworth, Derbyshire. DE4 4BL.

Cover sketch - "Somehwere in Sherwood Forest"
© Suncrest Ventures Ltd. 1994.

**An all British
product.**

## ABOUT JOHN N. MERRILL

Born in the flatlands of Bedfordshire he soon moved to Sheffield and discovered the joy of the countryside in the Peak District, where he lives. A keen walker who travels the world exploring mountains and trails. Over the last twenty years he has walked more than 150,000 miles - including the first walk around the entire coastline of Britain, 7,000 miles - and worn out over seventy pairs of boots. He has written more than 120 walk guides to areas in Britain and abroad, and created numerous challenge walks which have been used to raise more than £500,000 for charity. New Mexico, USA is his second home.

# CONTENTS

Page No.

# INTRODUCTION

For more than five years the idea of doing long walks in Nottinghamshire remained a book idea on my desk. Somehow, other books kept getting in the way. Eventually I made a stand and said it is next! For me, it was well worth the wait. I had already done short walk books to the Dukeries, South Notts and the Grantham Canal, so I had a basic layout of the countryside. But long walks allow you explore an area more fully and bring you to places only accessible on a long walk. For the last five months I have been walking the paths slowing piecing together my ideas and the ten walks in this book are my favourites.

Some of the walks are longer than usual but to shorten them would be to spoil their character; but what is a few more miles in such interesting country? The Chesterfield Canal has long been a favourite artery of mine and the two walks on it are outstanding. The one from Worksop - the longest walk in the book - is quite simply superb. I broke Sherwood Forest into three areas making three walks - north, middle and south; again absorbing walking. The River Trent makes an excellent segment to a walk and the one from Burton Joyce takes a lot of beating. Never having fully explored the river to the north of Newark, I have included one which is particulrly attractive. One walk explores a major section of the Grantham Canal in Nottinghamshire and includes some forest. The walk from Southwell passes through impressive hills and came as quite a surprise. My last walk was from Gotham and proved to be a magnificent route over hills and past attractive villages.

Nottinghamshire has much to offer the longer walker and I hope these walks give you greater insight into the diversity of the county. Apart from Creswell Crags and around Major Oak, I never saw another walker! These then are some outstanding long walks in Nottinghamshire and hope you enjoy them as much as I have exploring them.

*Happy walking!*
*John N. Merrill*

# WORKSOP - CHESTERFIELD CANAL - RETFORD - CLUMBER PARK - 18 or 23 MILES

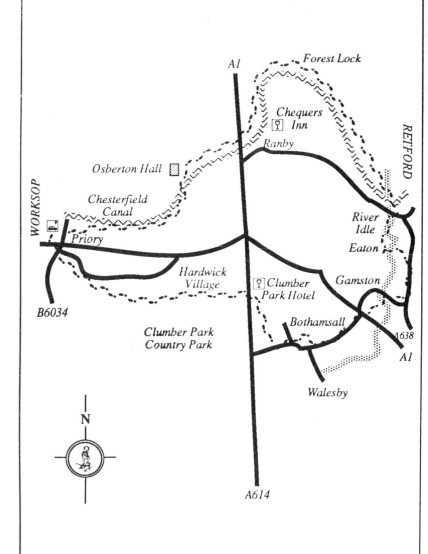

# WORKSOP -
## CHESTERFIELD CANAL
## - RETFORD
## - CLUMBER PARK
# - 18 or 23 MILES.
### - allow 7 to 9 hours.

*Worksop - Chesterfield Canal - Ranby - Retford - Eaton - Gamston - Bothamsall - Hardwick Village - Clumber Park - Worksop College - Worksop.*

 *- 1:50,000 Landranger Series Sheet No. 120 - Mansfield, Worksop & surrounding area.*
*1:25,000 Pathfinder Series Sheet Nos. SK47/57. SK 67/77. SK 68/78.*

*- Near Information/library. Near Worksop Priory.*

*Chequers Inn, Ranby; on the otherside of the canal but can be reached via Bridge a short distance ahead. Albert Hotel and others in Retford. Plough Inn, Gate Inn, Ordsall (Retford). Clumber Park Hotel. Numerous in Worksop at the end of the walk!*

**ABOUT THE WALK -** The longest in the book but a magnificent walk and basically flat all the way, to ease the mileage! My aim was simply to follow the Chesterfield Canal from Worksop to Retford (you can do it as a return walk of 18 miles) and then return to Worksop via Clumber Park. To do this you walk through two attractive villages and along the banks of the River Idle and have little over a couple miles of road walking. I had a perfect autumn day for the walk and saw only a couple of hikers on the canal. Then no one until Clumber Park and again only a couple out walking! The canal section from Ranby to Retford is particularly attractive and I saw a kingfisher on this stretch. I have started the walk from Worksop Priory.

**WALKING INSTRUCTIONS -** From Worksop Priory walk down the road past the church to a car park on your right. Here you can turn right and walk across the parkland to a lane, where turn left to gain the

Chesterfield Canal. Alternatively continue down the road to the canal and turn right along it. For the next 9 miles follow the path beside the canal. At first it is on your right, then after 2 miles crossover and keep it on your left to Osberton Lock. Here cross over and continue all the way to Retford with it in your right. After nearly 5 miles pass Ranby and the A1 road. Continue beside the canal past locks and bridges to Bridge No. 55. in Retford.

Continue along the canal past Asda supermarket on your left to a lock with a marina and Wharf Restaurant ahead. Turn right over the bridge at the lock and follow the passageway to Albert Road with the Albert Hotel on your left. Turn right along the road and after a short distance turn left along Victoria Road to the railway station. Turn left past it and walk through a subway under the railway to a road. Here turn left as footpath signed - "Ordsall". Follow the road then on a tarmaced path as you curve round to the road and church at the Ordsall area of Retford. Turn left past the church on your right to a road junction, opposite is the footpath and sign. The path is little used but keeps to the lefthand side of the field with a stream. Continue to a track, which cross and keep to the lefthand side of the field to a footbridge. Cross and continue along the field edge with a stream on your left to the road at Eaton with the River Idle on your left.

Turn left and walk through the village to the A638 road with Eaton Hall College on your left. Turn right and walk along the road for a mile to Rectory Lane, by Bramcote School into Gamston village. Follow the lane round to your right to the River Idle. Cross the road bridge and turn left immediately through the stile and walk along the embankment for 1/2 mile to a Pump House and track. Turn right and ascend the track to the B6387. Turn left and walk along this road for 1 1/2 miles, crossing the A1 and passing the entrance to Bevercotes Coal Mine on your left. Little over 1/4 mile later turn right onto a track to Haughton Park House - following a section of the Robin Hood Way. Approaching the house turn left along the track and follow this gated track to Bothamsall over 1/2 mile away.

Entering Bothamsall beside the church turn right along the road through the village and in 1/4 mile almost opposite a mound (a former Motte) turn right, as footpath signed. Cross the field to another and keep the hedge on your left as you aim towards some oil tanks. Here reach a track and turn right. Follow this to another and turn left. Keep straight ahead on this for more than a mile. Ignore are side turnings and the final 1/2 mile you are walking a footpath to the A614 road. Turn right and in a few yards opposite the Clumber Park Hotel, turn left into Clumber Park. Just past the gates turn right at the gate and path sign and follow the defined path across the field and down to the road close the ford before Hardwick Village. Cross the ford and walk through the village passing the telephone kiosk and war memorial cross. Keep on the road for nearly 1/4 mile to a bridlepath sign and path on your left. Turn left along the path through the woodland to a another road. Cross this, as guided by bridlepath signs, and continue on the path. Ignore the first turning right but take the second and in 1/4 mile gain the famous Lime Tree Avenue. Cross to another bridlepath sign and follow the path on the righthand side of a clearing to a bar post and track. Continue ahead on the track and in 1/2 mile pass a house on your right. Just after leave the track and follow a path just ahead through the woodland to open fields. Follow the defined path to woodland around Worksop College. Here bear right and follow the path just inside the woodland to Windmill Lane. Turn left along the lane past the college and Worksop Golf Course to the main road and roundabout. Cross over and follow the signed road - *"Low Town 1/2 mile"*. 3/4 mile down this reach the B6079 road in Worksop with the gatehouse of the Priory on your left. Turn left and in a few more strides you are back at the start after completing one of the finest walks in the area.

**WORKSOP PRIORY -** Dates from the 12th century. The main building has been restored but inside are an impressive array of paintings and monuments. One shows a skull with an arrow tip in it, a reminder of Sherwood Forest.

**OSBERTON HALL -** The original building dates from 1806 and designed by James Wyatt. Enlarged in 1853.

**CLUMBER PARK -** National Trust property. Clumber House was pulled down in 1938. The grounds and lakes are among the most visited of National Trust properties. The Lime Tree Avenue is one of the finest avenues in Europe.

*Osberton Lock.*

# RETFORD - CHESTERFIELD CANAL - LOUND AND RIVER IDLE - 14 MILES

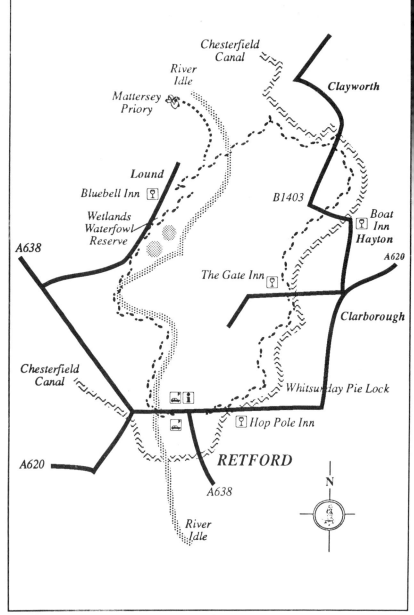

# RETFORD
## – CHESTERFIELD CANAL – LOUND AND RIVER IDLE – 14
# MILES
### – allow 5 hours.

●● ●● ●● *- Retford - Chesterfield Canal - Clayworth - River Idle - Lound - Chain Bridge Lane - Wetlands Waterfowl Reserve - River Idle - Retford.*

 *- 1:50,000 Landranger Series Sheet No. 120 - Mansfield, Worksop & surrounding area.*
*1:25,000 Pathfinder Series Sheet No. 745 (SK 68/78).*

 *- Chapelgate, Retford.*

⌖ *- Several in Retford. Hop Pole Inn, bridge 59 on canal. The Gate Inn, Clarborough, near Bridge No. 62. Boat Inn, Hayton, canal bridge No. 66. Bluebell Inn, Lound.*

---

**ABOUT THE WALK -** A really outstanding "water" walk. First you head northwards for six miles along the Chesterfield Canal to Clayworth. Here you cross fields to the River Idle, which you follow later, to reach the lane to Lound. From here you work your way past lagoons and the Wetlands Waterfowl Reserve to regain the River Idle which you follow back to Retford. A flat walk through a very interesting and scenic area. On nearing Lound you can extend the walk by four miles return walk, to visit the ruins of Mattersey Priory, founded in 1185, on the banks of the River Idle. Take your binoculars for you will see a wide variety of birds.

---

**WALKING INSTRUCTIONS -** Starting from Chapelgate car park in Retford, walk through the car park and archway to the road and shops. Turn along the road past the Information Centre on your right. Keep straight ahead on the road to the Chesterfield Canal, Grove Mill and Packet Inn. Turn left and follow the towpath, with the canal on your right and pass Grove Mill on your left. For the next 6 miles keep on the towpath to Clayworth and Bridge No. 68. After nearly 1 mile pass the Hop Pole Inn on your right and 1/4 mile later the Whitsunday Pie Lock. 1 1/2 miles later pass the Gate Inn, Clarborough on your left. Little over a mile later the Boat Inn at Hayton. The next three miles are quiet and nearing Clayworth the canal turns sharp left, near the Retford & Worksop Boat Club. Follow it round to Bridge No. 68 opposite Clayworth and a large hotel on your right.

Cross the bridge and follow the track round to your right for 1/4 mile to a stile and footpath sign on your left. Keep to the lefthand side of the field to a dyke. Cross this and bear half right across the field; the path is undefined. On the otherside of the field is a wooden footbridge. Over this the pathline is clearer and fenced. Keep straight ahead through sparse woodland to a metal bridge over the River Idle. On the otherside gain a track (Neatholme Road) which you follow for almost 2 miles to Lound. *(Extension to Mattersey Priory - After nearly a mile is a pathsign and stile on your right. By turning right here you pass between the lagoons and ascend to Wild Goose Farm. Walk through and gain a track. Turn right and follow a track to the River Idle. Follow the banks of the river to Mattersey Priory, little over a mile away. Return the same way.)* Continue on the track towards Lound; as you near the village you can turn left at a stile and path sign, which leads to Chain Bridge Lane. The only advantage of continuing into Lound is to visit the Blue Bell Inn! Reaching the road in the village turn left and just past the inn turn left again along Chain Bridge Lane. If on the path to the lane, turn left along the lane. Pass the office and works of Tarmac, Lound Quarry. Soon afterwards turn right along the first track on your right. Walk past Low Farm and on past Wetlands Waterfowl Reserve on your right to the minor road from Lound. Turn left to a stile and footpath sign - Retford - you have about 4 miles to go.

The path is defined at first but as you approach the former gravel pits area it is "lost". First walk beside the lagoon on your right, along a fenced path. Continue ahead at the end onto a track. Take the lefthand fork and follow this to the River Idle. Turn right and for the final 3 miles back to Retford, keep the river on your left as you walk along the embankment on a track and path. After 2 miles approach Bolham and a metal bridge over the river. Don't cross but follow the path along the banks of the river to the main road bridge in Retford - the tower of Retford church acts as a guide and is opposite Chapelgate car park. Walk under the bridge and ascend the steps to the road. Turn right and in a few yards right again to the church and car park.

*Mattersey Priory.*

**THE CHESTERFIELD CANAL** - The canal - 46 miles long with 65 locks - was completed on June 4th 1777 at a cost of £152,000. The construction of the Norwood Tunnel - 2,850 yards long - was a a major undertaking and in the long term brought about the demise of the canal, as it constantly needed attention and suffered from roof collapse and subsidence. In 1848 200,000 tons was being carried by the canal but ten years later it was half this amount. The railways took the business away and In 1908 the Norwood tunnel (nr. Worksop) was closed. The section from Worksop to West Stockwith and the River Trent is still in use by pleasure craft. The canal is slowly being restored and already a major section at the Chesterfield end has been restored. Whitsunday Pie lock - is named after a local farmer's wife who backed a large pie on Whit Sunday for the navvies.

**RETFORD** - Market town with an impressive outdoor market. Beside the cruciform church is a 24 pound canon captured at Sevastopol in 1855.

*The River Idle, between Lound and Retford.*

# CRESWELL CRAGS - SHERWOOD FOREST (NORTH) - 20 MILES

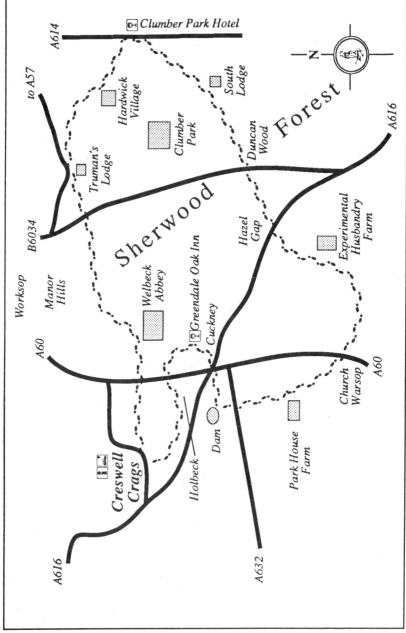

Clumber Park Hotel

A614

to A57

B6034

Hardwick Village

Clumber Park

Truman's Lodge

South Lodge

Duncan Wood

Forest

A616

Experimental Husbandry Farm

Hazel Gap

Sherwood

Worksop

Manor Hills

A60

Welbeck Abbey

Greendale Oak Inn

Cuckney

Church Warsop

A60

Holbeck

Dam

Park House Farm

Creswell Crags

A616

A632

# CRESWELL CRAGS - SHERWOOD FOREST (NORTH) - 20 MILES

## - allow 7 to 8 hours.

**• • • •** *- Creswell Crags Visitor Centre - Welbeck Estate - Truman's Lodge - Hardwick Village - Clumber Park Hotel - Robin Hood Way - South Lodge - Duncan Wood - A616 - Experimental Husbandry Farm - Church Warsop - Park House Farm - Cuckney - Welbeck Estate - Holbeck - Creswell Crags - Visitor Centre.*

 *- 1:50,000 Landranger Series Sheet No. 120 - Mansfield, Worksop & Surrounding area.*
*1:25,000 Pathfinder Series Sheet Nos. SK 47/57, SK 67/77, & SK 46/56.*

 *- Creswell Crags Visitor Centre. Note: Car park closes at 5.0p.m.*

 *Clumber Park Hotel, A614. Greendale Oak Inn, Cuckney.*

**ABOUT THE WALK** · A long one through *"Sherwood Forest"*, but being flat the miles float by! First you walk through the Welbeck Estate before encircling Clumber Park. You return through Church Warsop and the attractive village of Cuckney before regaining the Welbeck Estate. The final mile is through the Creswell gorge, along the southern side - Nottinghamshire. The car park closes at 5.0p.m. so you will have start early to complete the walk. A beautiful walk whatever the season.

**WALKING INSTRUCTIONS -** Starting from the Visitor's centre, walk down the drive/track away from it and in 1/2 mile reach the A60 road beside a lodge on your left. Cross over and walk along the drive into Welbeck Estate - you are now on the Robin Hood Way. Approaching a house on your right bear half left onto a concrete drive and follow it up and round to woodland. Entering turn left, as footpath signed, and walk around the edge of the woodland, passing a rugby field on your right. At the bottom gain a track and turn right and in a few yards turn left. 30 yards later turn left, as signed, and pass inbetween two lakes and ascend the lefthand side of the field to a gate and lodge. Go through onto a track/path and turn right. Now in forest follow the path gently ascending past an impressive beech area and through a sandstone gorge. Keep straight ahead following the path/track and in 1/2 mile from the gorge reach a lodge on your right. Continue ahead and in almost a mile another lodge. Continue straight ahead on the track and in 3/4 mile reach the B6034 road. Go straight across and continue on the track and in 1/2 mile reach a minor road. Turn right to Truman's Lodge and entrance to Clumber Park.

Turn left at the lodge and follow the road, as bridlepath signed. Keep on it for nearly a mile and take the second bridlepath on your right. Follow this track to another road. Cross over, as bridlepath signed, and follow the path for 1/4 mile before bearing left to reach the famed Lime Tree Avenue. Cross over to another path and signpost and in 200 yards reach the road to Hardwick Village. Turn right along it and walk through the village down and across the ford. Just after turn left and follow the path up and across the field to the road close to the A614 road, Turn left to it with the Clumber Park Hotel opposite.

Just before the road turn right and walk in the trees, parallelling the road. Cross a road and 1/4 mile later almost opposite a road on your left, turn right back into the forest proper; on your left are some picnic tables. For the next 3 miles keep straight ahead on this well defined path through Budby Corner Plantations. After 1 1/2 miles pass South Lodge on your right and 1/2 mile later reach the B6034 road at Duncan Wood Lodge. Cross over and continue on the defined path for nearly another mile to Hazel Gap and the A616 road. Go straight across, as signed, follow a path/track through Gleadthorpe Breck Plantation for 3/4 mile to a cross roads of track with the Experimental Husbandry Farm on your left. Turn left down the farm road to the minor road. Cross over with Gleadthorpe Grange on your right, and follow the farm drive then track and ascend to Budby South Forest. Entering the forest turn right and follow the path just inside it and in 1/4 mile pass impressive beech trees before open fields. Keep to the righthand side of the field and soon gain a track. Keep ahead and keep on the track and follow it round to your right then left to a sewage works. Here it turns right but, as signed keep ahead on a footpath across the field to a track. Turn right and descend to Burns Farm on your right and Church Warsop. Turn right then left along Manor Road and in 1/4 mile reach a road junction. Keep left along Eastlands Lane to the A60 road.

Turn right and pass the church on your left and just after is a footpath sign and stile on your left. Turn left and ascend the field to the far lefthand corner where there is a stile. Continue ascending to another stile and onto a corner of forest near an electric pole. Walk just inside the forest as you descend. Turn right then left at the bottom and continue descending on a good path to the farm road to Park House Farm. Keep ahead and follow the road to the A632 road 1/2 mile away.

Cross over to steps and stile and walk around the righthand side of a wooded mound. Descend to the track and Cuckney Dam. Turn right to the former mill, now a school, and walk along the lane to the A616 road. Keep right along the road - Ten Row - and cross the A60 road to reach the Greendale Oak Inn. Turn left down Norton Lane passing the church dedicated to St. Mary. At the bottom of the hill turn left at a stile and path sign and walk around the top of the field to a stile. Turn right and over this keep to the righthand side of the field to a minor road. Go straight across, as guided by signs and stiles and keep to the lefthand side of the field to reach the Welbeck Estate and lodge. Turn left along the tree lined drive and keep on it for the next mile, passing Park Lodge and a deer park on your right.

Turn left at the first road on your left to reach the A60 road by a lodge. Turn right and in 100 yards left along the lane towards Holbeck Woodhouse. Entering the village with shop on your left, keep ahead on the lane to Holbeck 1/2 mile away. Here on the left of the house is the path and sign for Creswell Crags. Cross a stile and guided by stiles cross the fields ascending with woodland on your right to a limestone outcrop, little over 1/2 mile away. Follow the path round and down to your right to enter Creswell Crags. Keep to the righthand side, thereby staying in Nottinghamshire, and pass the caves on your right and mill pond on your left. Follow the path round to your left at the end to the road. Go through the gate and turn right and descend the path back to the visitors centre.

**ROBIN HOOD WAY** - 88 mile route through Sherwood Forest from Nottingham Castle to Edwinstowe Church.

**CRESWELL CRAGS** - The limestone gorge is the border of Derbyshire and Nottinghamshire, and the Visitor's Centre is a joint project of both councils. The gorge has yielded some of the finest examples of fossils for the study of prehistoric man and man's evolution. The centre has a display of Stone Age man.

**WELBECK ABBEY** - is private and can be glimpsed as you walk along the bridleway. The buildings are now used by Welbeck College but are the work of the Dukes of Portland. Everything is on a grand scale; the riding school for instance, measures 385 feet long by 112 feet wide.

# EDWINSTOWE - 14 MILES
## - a walk in (middle) Sherwood Forest

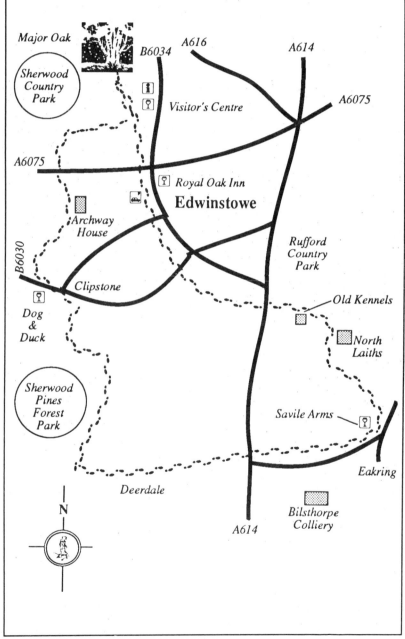

Major Oak

Sherwood Country Park

B6034

A616

A614

A6075

Visitor's Centre

A6075

Royal Oak Inn

Edwinstowe

Archway House

Rufford Country Park

B6030

Clipstone

Old Kennels

Dog & Duck

North Laiths

Sherwood Pines Forest Park

Savile Arms

Eakring

Deerdale

N

A614

Bilsthorpe Colliery

# EDWINSTOWE
# - a walk in (middle)
# Sherwood Forest
# - 14 miles
## - allow 5 to 6 hours.

**◖◗ ◖◗ ◖◗** - *Edwinstowe - Sherwood Country Park - Major Oak -*
*Birklands - A6075 - Archway House - Clipstone - Sherwood Pines*
*Forest Park - Deerdale - Robin Dam Bridge - Eakring - North Laiths*
*- Old Kennels - Rufford - Lidgett - Edwinstowe.*

 *- 1:50,000 Landranger Series Sheet No. 120 - Mansfield,*
*Worksop & Surrounding area.*
*- 1:25,000 Pathfinder Series Sheet No. SK 66/76 - Ollerton.*

*- Edwinstowe village. Sherwood Country Park & Visitor*

*Centre.*

🍷 *Dog & Duck, Clipstone. Saville Arms, Eakring. The Dukeries,*

*The Royal Oak, Edwinstowe.*

**ABOUT THE WALK** - This area of the "forest" is sparse but first you
walk through Sherwood Country Park and visit Major Oak. In the south
you explore Sherwood Pines Forest Park, before road walking to
Eakring. Here you cross the fields to Rufford and can visit Rufford
Country Park. Returning to Edwinstowe you can take the long way
round adding 1/2 mile extra to the walk. A delightful level walk in
Robin Hood country!

**WALKING INSTRUCTIONS** - Starting from Edwinstowe, walk
through the village to the Royal Oak Inn. Continue straight ahead on
the road past St. Mary's church to a car park on your left. Turn left past
the car park and cricket field. Here pickup the bridlepath signed -
Gleadthorpe and Major Oak. Enter Sherwood Forest Country Park and
after 1/2 mile you pass a track on your left, close to the southern edge
of the forest. This is your route but before following it continue ahead
following the signs to Major Oak, 1/4 mile ahead. *(If starting the walk
from the Visitors Centre, follow the signed path to Major Oak. Here turn
left along the track signed - Fairground/Edwinstowe village.)* Return to

the track, now on your right and turn right along it keeping close to the edge on the forest on your left. Keep on the track for 1 1/2 miles to a T junction with pine forest ahead. Turn left following a path/track and in 1/2 mile reach the A6075 road. Just before it turn right and follow a path just inside the trees for 1/4 mile to a track. Turn left to the road and cross it, and as bridlepath signed, follow the track, keeping to the righthand one to pass Archway House.

Continue on the track and pass under a railway bridge at Clipstone Junction West, and turn right along the track - Archway Road. Follow the "road" to the B6030 road opposite the Dog & Duck Inn. Turn left and pass under the railway and walk along the road for a 1/3 mile to the entrance to Sherwood Pines Forest Park. Walk along the road towards the car park, but just as you approach it keep right along the blue topped post walk route. In less than 1/4 mile it turns left. Follow it round and for the next 1 1/2 miles keep straight ahead on the forest track, ignoring all side routes and markers posts. The final 1/2 mile is following red topped posts (cycle route), with the bike on the reverse side of the post. Gain Eakring Road Car Park. Turn left along the road through Deerdale and in a mile reach the A614 road. Go straight across and in 100 yards pass the Robin Dam Bridge picnic site on your left; on your right is Robin Hood Farm. Keep on the road - Bilsthorpe Road - for 1 1/2 mile towards Eakring. Where the road turns sharp left to ascend Stonish Hill, is a footpath sign. Keep to the lefthand side of the field and in 1/4 mile gain the road again by a path sign. Continue along the road to the Saville Arms and Wellow Road, in Eakring.

Turn left along Wellow Road and towards the bottom of the hill just past a former Windmill on your right, turn left at a stile and path sign. Ascend to another before bearing right across the field to a track. Cross and continue ahead keeping to the left of a square plantation to a stile and path sign. Continue descending to a stile and bridge over the railway line. Cross and follow the path to a stile and footbridge over Gallow Hole Dyke. The pathline is faint across the next field but on the other side gain a track by a footpath sign and turn right along it. The track leads to the farm - North Laiths. Just before it turn left on a track and in over 1/2 mile pass the Old Kennels on your left. Just after pass a golf course on your right. Continue on the track to a junction; ahead is Rufford Country Park. Turn left and cross a foot-bridge and keep left along a track past a house. Just after turn right, as signed, and walk through woodland to Manor Farm and onto a lodge and A614 road.

Go straight across the road and walk along the track/road to road to Centreparcs. Walk along it a short distance before turning right along a track. 100 yards along here turn right and walk along the righthand side of the to Broadoak Brake. Approaching the woodland turn left and after a few yards right and follow the defined path along the righthand side of the field to the B6030 road, opposite South Forest; to your right is an inn! Cross the road and walk inbetween the houses to Rufford Road in Lidgett. Continue ahead along the road past the Dukeries Hotel back into Edwinstowe. You can at the B6030 road turn left and in 1/4 mile turn right past Holly Farm and follow the path down to another road. Cross over and cross a railway line and gain the path beside the River Maun. Turn right along it and in 1/4 mile reach a road and follow it to the main road. Turn left as signed - Major Oak 3/4 mile, and walk through Edwinstowe back to your start.

*Major oak.*

**MAJOR OAK** - The largest oak tree in England with a trunk 32 feet in circumference and whose branches spread to a diameter of 260 feet.

**ARCHWAY HOUSE** - A copy of the gatehouse to Worksop Priory and was built by the Duke of Portland in 1842; sometimes known as the Dukes folly.

**SHERWOOD FOREST** - Birklands means "birch lands". Sherwood Pines Forest Park is the largest forest park in the East Midlands and Britain's newest. Toilets and refreshments are available near the car park.

**EAKRING** - While just off route but well worth exploring. In 1670 the Rev. William Mompesson of Eyam (Peak District) came here. It was he who held the village together during the bubonic plague in 1665/6 when more than 300 died from the disease. As a result the people of Eakring made him live outside the village and hold services under an ash tree. Today close to the site is a memorial cross to the Pulpit Ash.

# BLIDWORTH - 17 MILES
## - a walk in (southern) Sherwood Forest.

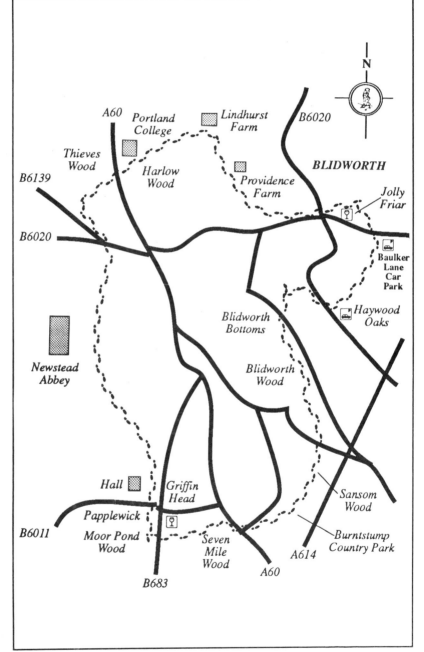

N

A60

Portland
College

Lindhurst
Farm

B6020

BLIDWORTH

Thieves
Wood

Harlow
Wood

Providence
Farm

Jolly
Friar

B6139

B6020

Baulker
Lane
Car
Park

Haywood
Oaks

Blidworth
Bottoms

Newstead
Abbey

Blidworth
Wood

Hall

Griffin
Head

Sansom
Wood

Papplewick

B6011

Moor Pond
Wood

Seven
Mile
Wood

A614

Burntstump
Country Park

B683

A60

# BLIDWORTH
## - a walk in (Southern) Sherwood Forest
# - 17 MILES
### - allow 6 to 7 hours.

■● ●● ●● *- Baulker Lane Car Park - Robin Hood Way - Blidworth - Providence Farm - Lindhurst Farm - Harlow Wood - Thieves Wood - B6020 - Newstead Abbey - Abbey Wood - Papplewick - Papplewick Dam - Seven Mile House - Burntstump Country Park - Sansom Wood - Blidworth Wood - Blidworth Bottoms - Haywood Oaks - Baulker Lane Car Park.*

**O.S. MAP** *- 1:50,000 Landranger Series Sheet No. 120 - Mansfield, Worksop & Surrounding area.*
*- 1:25,000 Pathfinder Series Sheet Nos. SK 45/55 and SK 65/75.*

**P** *- Baulker Lane Car Park - Sherwood Forest. Grid Ref 611559.*

**♀** *- Jolly Friar, Forest Folk, White Lion, Bird in the Hand, Blidworth. Griffin Head, Papplewick. Seven Mile House, A60.*

**ABOUT THE WALK -** A walk through the southern half of Sherwood Forest, with views to Newstead Abbey. In Thieves Wood you follow the "Great way of the King", the former route that linked Nottingham Castle with Bolsover and Tickhill castles. The eastern side through Sansom Wood back to Blidworth is surprisingly undulating countryside. There are several inns along the route and Newstead Abbey can be visited, combining to make a magnificent woodland hike.

**WALKING INSTRUCTIONS** - From the car park return to the road and turn left. In a few yards turn right and descend the forest track to the bottom and turn left - you are now following the Robin Hood Way. Keep straight ahead on the track to reach the minor road with the Jolly Friar Inn just ahead. Bear right along the road to the B6020 road in Blidworth, beside the Forest Folk Inn, 1/2 mile away. Turn left along the road and pass the White Lion Inn and another. Before the next one - Bird in the Hand - turn right, as footpath signed, and ascend steps to a stile. Keep to the righthand side of the field and descend to the edge of a small wood. It is well stiled and at the start on your left is a former windmill. Gaining the track by the wood, turn left and follow it and for the next 1/2 mile basically keep straight ahead, guided by stiles. This is horse country and climbing out of the shallow "dale", bear right across a field to a stile close to a hollow on your right. Continue diagonally right to two more stiles and reach a fenced path which brings you to a lane. Cross to your right to a bridlepath sign and walk along the track towards Providence Farm. Approaching the farm keep to the left of it, via a gate and descend to woodland and a footbridge. Cross and continue along the lefthand side of the field, on a track, heading for Lindhurst Farm.

Gaining the track here, turn left, and follow the track past the farm on your right and into Harlow Wood, 1/3 mile away. Entering the wood keep straight ahead for 100 yards and take the first track on your left. Follow this track for nearly a mile as it curves round to your right to the A60 road with Portland College on your right. Cross the road and continue on a track - now in Thieves Wood - and keep straight ahead for 1/2 mile to a "T" junction of tracks. Turn left and descend and in 100 yards, turn left following a path/track, part of the "Great way of the King." In 1/2 mile reach the B6139 road and car park. Turn left along the road to the B6020 road. Turn left along it for a few yards to a stile and fenced path on your right. Turn right and follow this to open fields with a former hospital on your right. Keep to the lefthand side of the field, on a path, and in little over 1/2 mile enter Abbey Wood. The path is defined and keeps close to a wooden fence on your right. Follow the path down to the drive to Newstead Abbey. Cross the road and continue on the path through the trees to a tarmaced lane. Keep ahead along it and to your right can be seen Newstead Abbey. Follow the road in woodland to a kissing gate by a former lodge. Continue ahead on a track and follow this for nearly a mile to the B683 road close to Papplewick Hall, to your right.

Turn right along the road, with the hall on your right. Walk through Papplewick to the cross roads beside the Griffin Head Inn. Cross over and keep ahead on the Manor Road (B683). In a few yards you can walk in woodland - Moor Pond Wood - around Papplewick Dam, but take the first exit on your left and continue on the road. Opposite the first road junction on your right to Hucknall, turn left, as footpath signed - Seven Mile House & Calverton. The path is defined and crosses the field to a track, where it turns slightly right and follows the line of electricity poles, past a large piggery to the track at Stanker Hill Farm. Basically go straight across, as signed, and walk along the edge on the field with the railway line on your right. 1/2 mile from the farm you reach the A60 road. Turn right and cross the railway line and just before Seven Mile House, turn left along the minor road, following signs for Burntstump Country Park. In 1/4 mile turn right, as signed, and walk through the edge of woodland to a hospital on your left; to your right is the Nottinghamshire Constabulary. Continue along the road to the Coun

-try Park car park. Exit it on the top righthand corner and follow the track beside a fence on your right to a minor road. Keep ahead on it and pass a rugby club on your right. Gain East Lodge and a minor road.

Turn left and in a few yards right along a No Through Road. Pass a couple of houses and continue on the track along the edge of woodland to a minor road. Turn right and follow the track in Sansom Wood. Keep on it for over 1/4 mile and ascend gradually. Take the first track on your left and soon start descending through the trees and cross a single tracked railway line and gain a minor road. Turn right and in 100 yards turn left into Longdale Lane Car Park. Basically keep straight ahead on the track and ignore all side tracks - the route is surprisingly hilly. In little over a mile reach a car park and picnic tables and road near Blidworth Bottoms. Turn left and just past Kirkfield Stables, turn right as footpath signed, and walk along a track. In 100 yards reach woodland and turn right and follow the track along the edge of the wood. In 1/4 mile turn left along a track and keep straight ahead on this track/path, ignoring all turnings, keeping to the lefthand edge of the wood. In just over 1/2 mile reach the road at Haywood Oaks. Turn left and in a few yards right into the forest car park. Keep to the lefthand side of the wood, again ignoring all turnings, following a bridleway and in 3/4 mile you are back at Baulker Lane car park.

**NEWSTEAD ABBEY -** Little of the 12th century Augustinian Priory remains, except for the west front. For nearly 300 years it was the home of the Byron family. In 1817 it was sold to meet the debts of the famous poet, Lord Byron. Since 1931 it has been owned by the Nottingham-shire City Council as a museum and the gardens are open to the public, from Easter to end of September.

**PAPPLEWICK HALL -** Built in 1787 for Sir Frederick Montagu, Lord of the Treasury, and designed by the Adam brothers. The nearby church of St. James is where Little John conducted the marriage ceremony of Alan-A-Dale, the minstrel to Robin Hood.

**SHERWOOD FOREST -** Once covered an area between 20 miles long by 8 miles wide, from Worksop to Nottingham. Today it is very fragmented. Harlow and Thieves Wood (named after the robbers who operated here), were part of the Royal Wood of Lyndhurst, owned by the King. Timber for Nottingham Castle came from here. Blidworth Wood was formerly known as "Assart Woods." Haywood Oaks is named after the oak trees that still remain here; some are centuries old.

# SOUTHWELL - 14 MILES

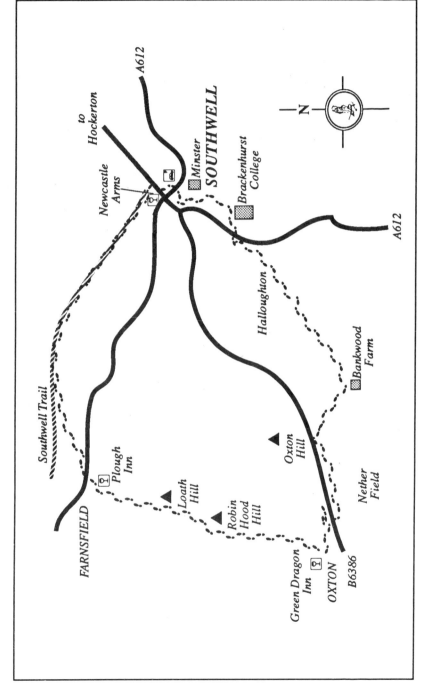

A612

to Hockerton

Newcastle Arms

Minster

SOUTHWELL

Brackenhurst College

A612

N

Haloughton

Bankwood Farm

Southwell Trail

Plough Inn

Loath Hill

Oxton Hill

Robin Hood Hill

Nether Field

FARNSFIELD

Green Dragon Inn

OXTON

B6386

# SOUTHWELL
# - 14 MILES
### - allow 4 1/2 hours.

■● ●■ ●■ *- Southwell - Brackenhurst College - Halloughton - Halloughton Dumble - Oxton Hill - Oxton - Robin Hood Hill - Combs Wood - Farnsfield - Southwell Trail - Southwell.*

 *- 1:50,000 Landranger Series Sheet No. 120 - Mansfield, Worksop & Surrounding area.*
*1:25,000 Pathfinder Series Sheet No. SK 65/75.*

 *- Southwell, opposite Minster.*

⚲ *- Saracens Head, The Reindeer, Newcastle Arms, Southwell; Green Dragon, Oxton; Plough Inn, Farnsfield.*

**ABOUT THE WALK -** Starting from the historic town of Southwell you cross the fields to the hills around Oxton. Here you ascend Robin Hood Hill, one of the finest vantage points in Nottinghamshire, and descend to Farnsfield. On the eastern side of the village you gain the Southwell Trail and follow it back to Southwell, where you have time to explore the Minster before returning home. An impressive scenic walk in central Nottinghamshire.

**WALKING INSTRUCTIONS -** From the car park turn right up the road to the road junction opposite the Saracens Head. Turn left along the Nottingham Road (A612). Just past the Reindeer Inn turn left, keeping on the A612 road. Pass the Leisure Centre on your left and soon afterwards take the first road (lane) on your left. Follow it round to your right and just past a house on your right is a gate and footpath sign. Keep to the lefthand side of the field to a stile and onto another near the A612 road. Bear left keeping the road on your right, over the hedge, to a stile with a small car park opposite. Turn left along the road and pass Brackenhurst College on your left. Continue along the road and take the second road on your right into Halloughton village. Keep on the lane for nearly a mile to a picnic site on your left close to the junction of the drive to Halloughton Wood Farm. Turn left along the concrete drive and approaching the farm keep left to a gate, as signed, and walk along the righthand side of the field with the farm on your right. Continue down the field to a footbridge over Halloughton

Dumble. Cross to your left and keep to the righthand side of the field and pass a ruined farm. Continue ahead, now on a track to a major track and gate. Here turn right and walk through Bankwood Farm and continue on the farm drive/track to the B6386 road, little over a mile away.

Turn left and follow the minor road for 1 1/4 miles. Soon descend Oxton Hill (121m), with Nether Field on your left. Take the first road on your right - Blind Lane - and walk into the village of Oxton. Just before the Green Dragon Inn, turn right along Windmill Hill Lane; signed "Farnsfield 4 1/4 miles." Ignore all turnings, keeping straight ahead and ascend the hedged track towards Robin Hood Hill. At the end of the track keep straight ahead across the field to a stile with prominent "hills" (earthworks) ahead. Keep to the lefthand side of them to reach another stile and path signs close woodland, with Loath Hill (144m) above. Walk around the edge of the wood and descend to your left to a track. Turn left along it to a minor road. Go straight across as stiled and signed and keep along the field edge before turning right keeping the field hedge on your left as you aim for Combs Wood. Gaining the wood turn left as signed - "Farnsfield 2 miles." Follow the track on the edge of the wood round to your right to a stile. Cross this and enter the wood and follow a defined path through it to another stile and path sign. Cross the field well to the right a house to a footpath sign and track. Turn right along the track which soon becomes a lane as you approach Farnsfield. Gaining the houses turn right along Quaker Lane and follow it round to your right then left to the main road in the village.

Turn right pass the Plough Inn and left along Brickyard Lane. Little over 1/2 mile along here you gain the Southwell Trail on your left. Follow this trail to your right for more than 4 miles to Southwell. In little over a mile cross the roads to Kirklington and 1 1/2 mile later the road to Maythorne. Continue of the trail for more than a mile to its end at Station Road. Turn right and pass the Newcastle Arms and gain a cross roads. Cross over and continue along Burbage and into central Southwell. You soon gain the Saracens Head Inn and turn left down to the car park and the Minster opposite.

**SOUTHWELL** - The Minster dates from 1108 with further work in the 13th Century, especially the Chapter House in 1295 which is world renowned for its stone carvings, particularly the "Leaves of Southwell." The nave is impressive with huge Norman arches. Adjacent to the Minster are the ruins of the 15th Century Archbishop's Palace. The Saracens Head is where Charles Stuart spent his last hours as a free man before surrounding to the Scots at Kelham.

**HALLOUGHTON** - The church although rebuilt last century has a fine 15th Century screen. Entering the village on your left is a solid tower and now incorporated into a house. The tower is all that remains of a 14th Century house associated with a Canon from Southwell Minster.

**OXTON** - Well worth exploring. The church dates back to the 13th Century and has many monuments to the Sherbrooke family. The earthwork - Oldox Camp - on Robin Hood Hill, is a magnificent vantage point over Mansfield and Sherwood Forest.

**SOUTHWELL TRAIL** - Former railway line between Southwell and Bilsthorpe.

*Southwell Minster.*

29

# BURTON JOYCE AND
# THE RIVER TRENT - 17 MILES

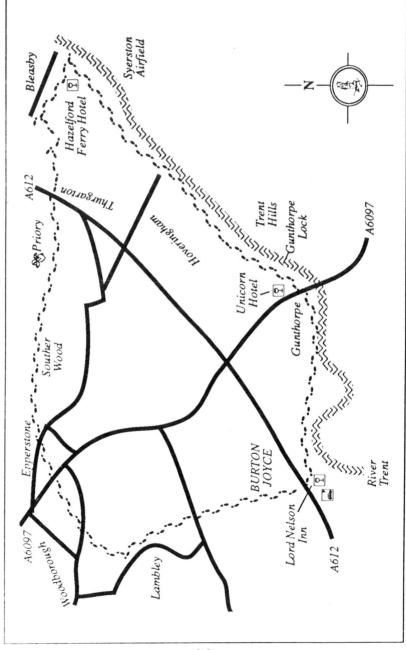

# BURTON JOYCE
# AND THE
# RIVER TRENT
# - 17 MILES
## - allow 6 to 7 hours.

*Burton Joyce (Lord Nelson Inn) - River Trent - Gunthorpe Lock - River Trent - Hazelford Ferry Hotel - Bleasby - Thurgarton - Souther Wood - Eastwood Farm - Hagg Lane - Epperstone - A6097 - Woodborough - Lambley - Burton Joyce.*

*- 1:25,000 Pathfinder Series Sheet No. 813 (SK 64/74) - Carlton and Elston.*

*- Roadside parking beside The Roberts Recreation Ground, on Chestnut Grove, near Lord Nelson Inn, Burton Joyce. Grid Ref. 648437.*

*- Lord Nelson Inn, Burton Joyce. Anchor Inn, Tom Brown & Unicorn Hotel, Gunthorpe. Hazelford Ferry Hotel. Wagon & Horse, Bleasby. Coach & Horses and Red Lion Inn, Thurgarton. Cross Keys Inn, Epperstone. Woodborough and Lambley, one just off the route.*

**ABOUT THE ROUTE -** An exceptional walk! First you walk beside the River Trent for almost 7 miles to Hazelford Ferry. Here you walk inland to return through villages, across fields and woodland back to Burton Joyce. I first did this walk one winters day and saw few people despite being hardly a cloud in the sky. Near Hazelford Ferry I sat on the river bank and ate my first bar of chocolate of the day; by the time I returned to Burton Joyce another three had been consumed! The river is active during the summer months with cruisers and narrowboats passing. Gunthorpe Lock is fascinating when a boat passes through. The views as you cross the valleys back are extensive.

**WALKING INSTRUCTIONS -** From the Roberts Recreation Ground walk down the No Through Road past the Lord Nelson Inn and cross the railway line. Continue ahead across a track and onto the banks of the River Trent and turn left. For the next 7 miles keep the river on your right. In little over 1/2 mile pass the 13km marker - when you pass the 23km marker you know you will be leaving the river! Nearly 3 miles from Burton Joyce, walk under the A6097 bridge and reach Gunthorpe. Continue beside the river past the marina and onto Gunthorpe Lock, with the Trent Hills opposite. Another 2 1/2 miles and you gain the road near Hoveringham and walk along it past the Old Elm Tree inn (now a private house) on the corner. Here continue ahead beside the river for another 2 1/2 miles to pass the 23km marker. Shortly afterwards reach the Hazelford Ferry Hotel on your left. Here leave the riverside and turn left along the lane.

At the cross roads, 1/3 mile later, go straight across into the village of Bleasby. Pass St. Mary's church and Wagon & Horses Inn on your right. Almost a 1/3 mile later and before the railway crossing turn left, as footpath signed, beside Manor Cottage. Walk along the tarmaced surface to Bleasby Primary School. Where it turns right keep ahead to a gate and now follow a defined path around the edge of the fields, guided by stiles. After the third stile the path turns right along the field edge to the railway line. Don't cross it; turn left and follow the path close to it. Pass a lake on your left and just after turn right across the railway and follow a track towards Thurgarton village. 1/4 mile along here the track divides; take the lefthand one. 100 yards later turn right and follow a path to a kissing gate and onto the road in the village, by a footpath sign. Turn left and pass the Coach & Horses Inn to a T Junction - to your right is the Red Lion Inn. Turn left and in 20 yards turn right at the entrance to Thurgarton Priory and St. Peters church. Here on the left is the bridlepath signed - Epperstone, your next destination.

The path/track is defined and zig-zags up the field before turning left to the field boundary. Here turn right keeping the hedge on your left as you walk along the "ridge" with views to Thurgarton Priory. The path is well gated and in a mile approach Souther Wood. Follow the path round to your right to a gate and walk through an arm of the wood to another gate. Turn left and walk around the edge of the wood to a track. Turn left and follow the track with the wood on your left towards Hagg Farm less than 1/4 mile away. Nearing the farm turn right on a track to the edge of Thistly Coppice. Turn left with the wood on right. Follow the path/track beside the wood and in 150 yards turn right on a track, still with the wood on your right. You soon leave the wood and continue on the track to the right of Eastwood Farm. Here gain Hagg Lane and turn left and follow the lane past the farm and descend to the lane to the main Epperstone village road, beside a bridlepath sign.

Turn right and walk through the village with a Dovecote in a field on your left. Pass the Cross Keys Inn on your right and take the second lane on your left - Bland Lane. Follow this to the end and turn right and walk past the houses to a stile; as footpath signed. Cross to another stile and continue across the field to a stile and footbridge over Grimesmoor Dyke. Continue to more footbridges and keep to the lefthand side of The Old Mill to gain the A6097 road, via a stile. Turn right and in a few yards left, as footpath signed. Cross the stile and cross the field to another. Continue ahead and soon keep a hedge on your left and reach a metal clad shed. Pass it on the right and 50 yards later turn left and walk up the field to Lowdham Lane.

Turn right towards Woodborough. In less than 1/4 mile on the outskirts of the village turn left, as bridlepath signed - Lowdham 3 miles. Cross a stile and onto a gate and tarmaced drive towards a caravan site. Basically walk up the shallow valley keeping the field boundary on your right. The route is well defined and gated. In 2/3 mile with some trees on your right, keep straight ahead to a path junction close to Green Lane. Turn right then left walking close to the hedge and Green Lane on your right. At the end of the field with a grass runway on your left reach a stile. Over this turn right to Green Lane. Turn left and almost immediately left again and follow a hedge path on your left. This keeps to the righthand side of the fields and follow it round the field edges, with the houses of Lambley on your right and straight ahead. On your left in the middle of the field can be seen a prominent mound. Follow the path down and around the field to a stile. Here turn right to another and bear left across the field with a pond on your left. At the end gain the minor road on the outskirts of Lambley village.

Cross over to a track and bridlepath sign - Burton Joyce. Turn right then left along the track and ascend over the field and descend towards Burton Joyce. Basically keep straight ahead as the track becomes tarmaced and known as Bridle Road. At all road crossings keep straight ahead and in 2 miles cross a road in Burton Joyce and continue along Lambley Lane to the A612 road. Turn left and in a few yards is St. Helens Church and the Robert Recreation Ground on your right.

**THURGARTON PRIORY -** Founded by Ralph d'Eyncourt. Much of the remaining church, dedicated to St. Peter, dates from the 13th century. The hall which occupies much of the site was built by John Gilbert Cooper.

# CARLTON-ON-TRENT AND THE RIVER TRENT - 12 MILES

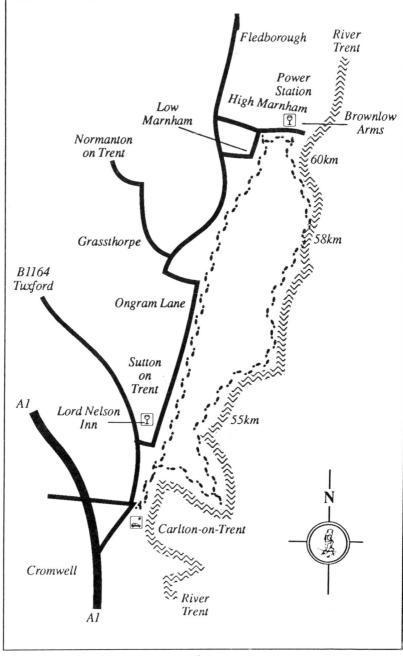

Fledborough

River Trent

Power Station

High Marnham

Low Marnham

Brownlow Arms

60km

Normanton on Trent

58km

Grassthorpe

B1164 Tuxford

Ongram Lane

55km

Sutton on Trent

A1

Lord Nelson Inn

Carlton-on-Trent

N

Cromwell

A1

River Trent

# CARLTON-ON-TRENT AND THE RIVER TRENT
# - 12 MILES
### - allow 4 to 5 hours.

*- Carlton -on-Trent - River Trent - High Marnham - Low Marnham - Sutton on Trent - Carlton-on-Trent.*

 *1:25,000 Pathfinder Series Sheet Nos. 764 and 781 (SK 86/ 96) - Lincoln (South).*

*- No official one. Roadside parking near St. Mary's church, Carlton-on-Trent.*

*- Brownlow Arms, High Marnham. Lord Nelson Inn, Sutton on Trent.*

**ABOUT THE WALK -** I met no one on this walk - just peace and solitude. A flat but interesting walk to the north of Newark along the banks of the River Trent. I saw cormorants, grey heron and Canada Geese but no boats! The villages are quiet and outstanding with attractive halls and churches and worth exploring. Although one of the shortest walks in this book, I wanted to explore the river off the beaten track and was delighted to find such an unspoilt area.

**WALKING INSTRUCTIONS -** Starting from St. Mary's church in Carlton-on-Trent, walk northwards past the hall dated 1765 (to view phone 0636 - 821421) on your left and the Dower House on your right. Just after turn right on the No Through Road. Follow it round to Mill Farm and the tall sail-less windmill. Go through a gate and walk along the top of the river bank and for the next six miles basically keep beside the river, on your right. After nearly 2 miles you seem to have made little progress as the river doubles back on it self. Just past the windmill on the other bank is the 52 km marker; when you pass the 60 km marker you know you will soon be leaving the river. In the distance can be seen a power station and again once you get close to it, this is where you leave it. Here you gain a road and turn left along it past the

Brownlow Arms and into High Marnham. Entering the village you can cross the fields to your left past the house and alongside a wood to the road again, as stiled and signed. Alternatively you can continue to the road junction and turn left and soon pass a stile and path sign on your left.

Continue on the lane to Low Marnham and its church dedicated to St. Wilfred, 1/2 mile away. Walk through the churchyard to the road on the otherside and path sign. The path is little used and is mostly all there. Walk past Church Farm on your right and onto the top of a dike. Here a path goes to your right, but your route is straight ahead. Cross the field to a stile and footbridge. Cross and bear right along the field edge with a drainage channel on your right. Pass a pine plantation on your right and continue along the field edge to a track - Holme Lane. Cross to a footpath sign and straight across the field to a gate, slightly to your left. Here turn right with a drainage channel on your left and reach Ingram Lane. Turn left along the narrow lane and follow it round to your right and on to Sutton on Trent more than a mile away. Keep straight ahead through the village, past All Saints church, the Old Bakehouse and the Lord Nelson Inn. Just after the road turns right. Here on the bend keep straight ahead on Carlton Lane, a No Through Road. In 3 /4 mile enter Carlton-on-Trent and your starting out route. Retrace your steps back to St. Mary's church.

Carlton -on -Trent is worth exploring. The old Forge has a large stone horseshoe with a notice -

*Gentlemen as you pass by upon
this shoe, pray cast an eye.
If it be too strait I'll make it
wider, I'll ease the horse and
please the rider. If lame from
shoeing as they often are,
you may have then eased with
The Greatest Care.*

*River Trent and old Mill near Carlton on Trent.*

*Gunthorpe Lock, River Trent - Burton Joyce walk.*

# COTGRAVE & THE GRANTHAM CANAL - 13 MILES

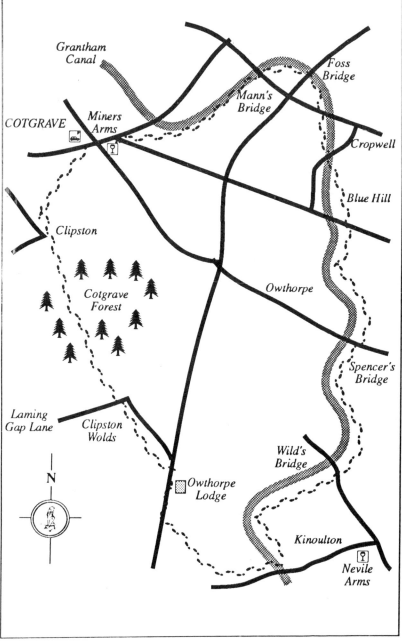

Grantham Canal

Foss Bridge

Mann's Bridge

COTGRAVE

Miners Arms

Cropwell

Blue Hill

Clipston

Cotgrave Forest

Owthorpe

Spencer's Bridge

Laming Gap Lane

Clipston Wolds

N

Owthorpe Lodge

Wild's Bridge

Kinoulton

Nevile Arms

# COTGRAVE & THE GRANTHAM CANAL - 13 MILES
## - allow 5 hours.

*- Cotgrave - former Grantham Canal - Kinoulton - Black's Farm - Kinoulton Gorse - Owthorpe Lodge - Wynnstay Wood - Clipston Wolds - Cotgrave Forest - Clipston on the Wolds - Cotgrave.*

 *- 1:25,000 Pathfinder Series Sheet No. 834 (SK 63/73) - Radcliffe on Trent & Keyworth.*

*Roadside parking in Cotgrave beside All Saints church, on Church Lane. Grid Ref. 644354.*

*- Maners Arms, Cotgrave. Nevile Arms, Kinoulton - 1/2 mile from route.*

**ABOUT THE WALK -** From Cotgrave you walk along a major section of the old Grantham Canal - 6 miles - to Kinoulton. You pass old locks, waterfilled sections, and dry ones, and see a lot of wild fowl. In its heyday the canal must have been impressive meandering through rolling countryside. From Kinoulton you cross the fields and woodland to reach the "wolds" and Cotgrave Forest, before descending back to Cotgrave.

**WALKING INSTRUCTIONS -** Starting from All Saints church in Cotgrave, turn right along the main road past the Maners Arms and Methodist church. In 1/4 mile the road turns sharp right, keep straight ahead on the road to Straglethorpe - Hollygate Lane. Little over 1/4 mile along here reach Hollygate Bridge and the Grantham Canal. Turn right along the towpath with the canal on your left; keep beside the canal for the next 6 miles to Kinoulton. The River Trent is 5 1/2 miles to your left and Cropwell Bishop 3 1/2 miles to your right. As you walk along the can you see many mileposts stating the distance from the River Trent. Pass two locks and in 3/4 mile Mann's Bridge. Another 3/4 mile and you are at Foss Bridge No. 18 and two more locks. 1 mile later gain Cropwell Bridge near Cropwell Bishop - Cotgrave 3 miles/ Kinoulton 3 1/2 miles. Continue with the canal on your left past a Gypsum Pit on your right to the next road 1/4 mile away. Cross over and now keep the canal on your right for the remainder of the canal section to Kinoulton over 3 miles away. The canal is now waterfilled and once you have passed the mile post - 11 1/2 miles from the Trent - Kinoulton is just ahead. Gain the road and bridge No. 28 at Kinoulton and turn right along the road - to your left 1/2 mile away is the Nevile Arms.

Walk along the road for more than 1/4 mile to the outskirts of the village, to where the road turns sharp left beside Corner Cottage. Turn right to a stile and footpath sign. Keep to the edge of the field and cross another to a field boundary bearing left up towards a wood. Walk along the righthand side of the field to the wood. Turn right and walk beside the wood - Kinoulton Gorse - on your left for more 1/4 mile. Where it turns sharp left, turn left then right and follow a track along the edge of the field to A46 road. Turn right and pass Owthorpe Lodge and a few yards later turn left along the lane - Laming Gap Lane - and pass Wynnstay Wood on your left. 3/4 mile from the A46 the lane turns sharp left, here keep straight ahead on a track beside Cotgrave Forest. Follow the track down to more forest and turn right then left and continue on the track. Keep straight ahead on the track through the forest and in just over 1/2 mile leave it now walking along Wolds Lane. Follow it to the village of Clipston 1/2 mile away. Gaining the road keep straight ahead on it out of the village and follow it round to your right. Where it turns left keep right on a track through woodland. Continue on it down to the end of the field. Turn left and in a few yards turn right and walk beside the hedge on your left. At the end of the field continue ahead across the field to the houses of Cotgrave. Reaching the road - White Furrows - turn left and follow it round to the main road. Turn left and keep straight ahead, soon walking along Scrimshire Lane. At the end with the junction with Plumtree Road turn right to All Saints church and start of the walk.

**GRANTHAM CANAL** - In November 1791 the capital - £40,000 - was raised at a single meeting for the construction of the canal from the River Trent at Nottingham to Grantham - 33 miles. The canal was a useful waterway last century but like so many suffered badly from rail competition. In 1905 18,802 tons were carried and by 1924 this had dwindled to 1,583 tons. Five years later in 1929 it was closed. Today it is sadly derelict with many bridges now gone, sections without water and badly overgrown; and other sections particularly attractive and well preserved as this walk shows. The Grantham Canal Restoration Society have placed information plaques where a road crosses the canal. Considerable work is now being carried out restoring the canal; the locks near Woolsthorpe have been restored in 1994.

*Grantham Canal near Cropwell.*

*Lime Tree Avenue, Clumber Park - Worksop walk.*

# THE HILLS OF GOTHAM
## - 19 MILES

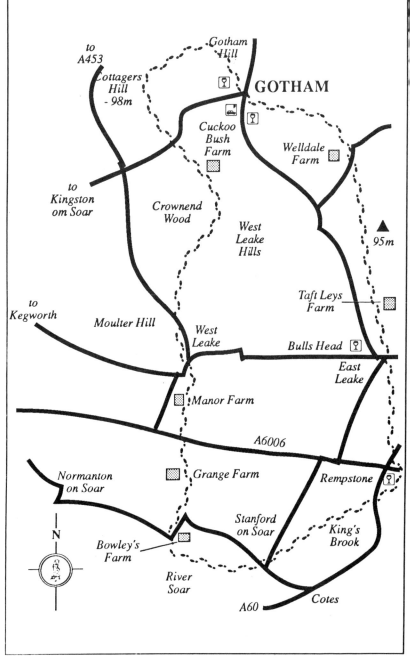

to A453

Cottagers Hill - 98m

Gotham Hill

GOTHAM

Cuckoo Bush Farm

Welldale Farm

to Kingston om Soar

Crownend Wood

West Leake Hills

95m

to Kegworth

Moulter Hill

West Leake

Taft Leys Farm

Bulls Head

East Leake

Manor Farm

A6006

Normanton on Soar

Grange Farm

Rempstone

Stanford on Soar

King's Brook

N

Bowley's Farm

River Soar

Cotes

A60

# THE HILLS OF GOTHAM
# - 19 MILES
### - allow 7 hours.

■● ●● ●● *- Gotham - Welldale Farm - Trig Point 95m. - Taft Lays Farm - East Leake - Sheepwash Brook - Rempstone - Sutcliffe Hill - King's Brook - Stanford on Soar - Fox Hill - Bowley's Farm - Grange Farm - A6006 - Manor Farm - West Leake - Moulter Hill - Crownend Wood - Cuckoo Bush Farm - Cottagers Hill - Gotham Hill - Gotham.*

 *- 1:25,000 Pathfinder Series Sheets No. 853 (SK 42/52) - Loughborough (North) and Castle Donington.*

*- Beside Gotham church, opposite the Sun Inn.*

*- The Windmill, The Sun Inn, Cuckoo Bush Inn, Gotham. Bulls Head, East Leake (just off the route). White Lion Inn, Rempstone. Star Inn, West Leake (1/2 mile from route.)*

**ABOUT THE WALK -** To the south of Nottingham upto the Leicestershire boundary are a range of gentle hills with picturesque villages. This walk encircles the area, crossing many "hills" on well defined paths and bridleways. I saw no other walker despite being a sunny day. Skylarks sung in the air and in one wood I watched a blue tit, robin and a tree creeper exploring a tree. Much of the route was new to me and it came as a pleasant surprise at how attractive the area is. The southern tip of the walk from Rempstone to Stanford on Soar, you walk along the Leicestershire bank of King's Brook.

**WALKING INSTRUCTIONS -** From the Square and church in Gotham turn left along Moor Lane and follow it for 1/4 mile to a track and bridlepath sign on your right. Follow the track and in 1/4 mile keep left and follow the track round to your left with the remains of an old railway on your right. In 1/2 mile turn right, as signed, and left keeping to the lefthand side of the field. Follow the field round to your right to a footbridge and bridlepath sign. Here turn left and basically aim towards the tunnel in the railway ahead. Walk through the tunnel and continue on a track. Keep a hedge on your right and Welldale Farm to your right. 1/4 mile from passing the farm turn right at a stile and diagonally cross two fields to the road near the farm drive, where there is a stile and path sign. Turn right and pass the farm and just after turn left, as bridlepath signed, and follow the hedged track round and up over the hill, passing trig point 95m. just to your left, near Hill Top Farm. Continue on the track and descend to Taft Leys Farm and T junction. Turn right and in a few yards left at a gate. Cross the field to the far righthand corner where there is a stile. Continue across the next field to a stile and turn left and soon gain the footbridge over the Kingston Brook. Bear partly right across the field to a stile on the edge of the houses. Cross this and walk around the house before bearing left to a stile and road at East Leake, close to the playing field.

Turn right then left along Castle Hill and in less than 1/2 mile near the end of the houses, turn left along Mill Lane. A short distance along here go through the stile on your right and walk past the lefthand side of Manor Farm, guided by stiles. Past the farm continue on a defined path to a footbridge over Sheepwash Brook. Cross over and continue ahead to a stile. Here the path turns left to pass a lake on your left and a few solitary gravestones on your right (see notes at end). Just after gain a stile and large field. Using Rempstone's church tower, dedicated to All Saints, as a guide cross the field towards it to a stile and path sign. Continue along the road to its junction with the A60. Cross over and walk through the village and just past the White Lion Inn, turn right at the stile and footpath sign - Hoton 3/4 mile. Ascend to the top of the rise and turn right over Sutcliffe Hill and descend to the A60 road. Turn left along it for a few yards, stepping into Leicestershire, and turn right, as footpath signed, and follow the path beside the King's Brook. For the next 2 1/2 miles the path keeps close to the brook on your right. It is well signed and the path is frequently used and to your right can be seen Stanford Hall. After nearly an hours walking reach the road and bridge just south of Stanford on Soar.

Turn right and walk past the impressive church on your left and into the hamlet. Opposite the Post Office is the footpath sign on your left but the stile is a little further ahead! Walk along the righthand side of the field towards the former course of the River Soar with a footbridge. Don't cross it but turn right over a stile and soon cross a railway line and onto Fox Hill. Lovely views from here of the river as you descend to its banks. Continue beside it towards another railway line. Approaching it bear right to a stile and cross over and turn right and soon gain a bend in the minor road to Normanton on Soar. Turn right along the road and cross the railway and pass Bowley's Farm on your right. Just after the road turns right, here on your left is a bridlepath sign and defined path. Keep to the lefthand side of the field and in 1/2 mile bear left, now on a track to gain Grange Farm. Walk through the farm and turn right, continuing on the bridlepath on the lefthand side of the field, heading towards woodland. Go through a gate and ascend through the trees on a wide path to the A6006 road.

Go straight across to a stile and bridlepath sign. Continue ahead and start descending will Hills Farm on your right. The route is defined and well gated. Descend to a minor road. Cross to a stile and ascend to Manor Farm. Here gain a track and follow it down to a minor road. Just before it turn left, as signed and stiled, and reach another stile. Here turn right and cross the footbridge over Kingston Brook. Bear slightly left to the stile with metal rail and church of West Leake. Walk through the churchyard to the road and turn left. In a few yards at the road junction turn right and ascend the road for 1/2 mileover Moulter Hill. Just as you start to descend turn right, as bridlepath signed, and follow the track which leads to Crownend Wood, more than a mile away. Ascend between the plantations to a gate and track from Cuckoo Bush Farm on your right. Turn left and descend the track to a minor road more than 1/2 mile away. Gotham can be seen below, but you have more than 2 miles to walk before your get there!

Cross the road and ascend the track beyond leading to the top of Cottagers Hill - 98m. Here beside a solitary oak turn right, as bridlepath signed, and walk along the crest of the ridge with woodland on your left. Continue to a gate and on to Gotham Hill with views to Attenborough Nature Reserve, to the north. Gaining a gate and more woodland turn right and start descending beside the woodland before leaving it and descending to a gate. Through this turn right onto a track which leads down to Gotham. Keep straight ahead through the village back to the Square and church where you began, ending an exceptional walk.

**GOTHAM -** Renowned for the Tales of Gotham and the Cuckoo Bush Inn retains the name to one of the stories. The church dates from the 13th century and the broach spire is one of the earliest stone spires in the country.

**REMPSTONE -** The present church dates from 1771 with much of the stone coming from the earlier church. As you crossed the fields to here you passed several solitary gravestones which is all that remains of the earlier church, known as St. Peter in the Rushes.

**STANFORD ON SOAR -** Nottinghamshire most southerly point. The church dates from the 13th century. The village was rebuilt by the Ratcliffs and their name and emblem can be seen on the buildings.

# WALK
# RECORD
# CHART

**Date walked -**

## _WALKS -_

_WORKSOP & CHESTERFIELD CANAL - 18 or 23 MILES_ ....................

_RETFORD & CHESTERFIELD CANAL - 14 MILES_ ............................

_SHERWOOD FOREST - NORTH - CRESWELL CRAGS - 20 MILES_ ..........

_SHERWOOD FOREST - MIDDLE - EDWINSTOWE - 14 MILES_ ............

_SHERWOOD FOREST - SOUTH - BLIDWORTH - 17 MILES_ ................

_SOUTHWELL - 14 MILES_ ....................................................

_BURTON JOYCE & RIVER TRENT - 17 MILES_ ...................................

_CARLTON-ON-TRENT & RIVER TRENT - 12 MILES_ ...........................

_COTGRAVE & THE GRANTHAM CANAL - 13 MILES_ ..........................

_THE HILLS OF GOTHAM - 19 MILES_ .................................................

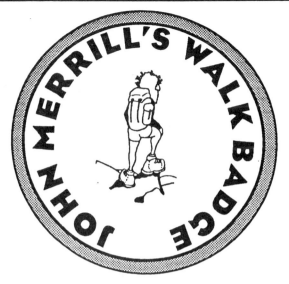

## THE JOHN MERRILL WALK BADGE

Complete six of the walks in this book and get the above special John Merrill badge and signed certificate. Badges are blue cloth with lettering and walking man embroidered in four colours and measure 3 1/2" diamater.

## ( BADGE ORDER FORM )

Date and details of walks completed........................................................................

..............................................................................................................................

NAME ...................................................................................................................

ADDRESS .............................................................................................................

..............................................................................................................................

Price: £3.00 each including postage, VAT and signed completion certificate.
Amount enclosed (Payable to El Morro Equipment Ltd) ..

From: El Morro Equipment Ltd.,
Milne House, Speedwell Mill, Millers Green,
Wirksworth,, Derbyshire. DE4 4BL.
℃ /**Fax** (0629) 826354 - 24hr answering service.
\*\*\*\*\*\*\*\*\*\*\*\* *YOU MAY PHOTOCOPY THIS FORM* \*\*\*\*\*\*\*\*\*

## "I'VE DONE A JOHN MERRILL WALK" T SHIRT -

Emerald Green with white lettering and walking man logo. Send £7.50 to El Morro
Equipment Ltd., stating size required.

### John Merrill's "Happy Walking!" Cap - £3.00

# ABOUT THE WALKS

Whilst every care is taken detailing and describing the walk in this book, it should be borne in mind that the countryside changes by the seasons and the work of man. I have described the walk to the best of my ability, detailing what I have found on the walk in the way of stiles and signs. Obviously with the passage of time stiles become broken or replaced by a ladder stile or even a small gate. Signs too have a habit of being broken or pushed over. All the route follow rights of way and only on rare occasions will you have to overcome obstacles in its path, such as a barbed wire fence or electric fence. On rare occasions rights of way are rerouted and these ammendments are included in the next edition.

The seasons bring occasional problems whilst out walking which should also be borne in mind. In the height of summer paths become overgrown and you will have to fight your way through in a few places. In low lying areas the fields are often full of crops, and although the pathline goes straight across it may be more practical to walk round the field edge to get to the next stile or gate. In summer the ground is generally dry but in autumn and winter, especially because of our climate, the surface can be decidedly wet and slippery; sometimes even gluttinous mud!

These comments are part of countryside walking which help to make your walk more interesting or briefly frustrating. Standing in a farmyard up to your ankles in mud might not be funny at the time but upon reflection was one of the highlights of the walk!

The mileage for each walk is based on three calculations -

1. pedometer reading.
2. the route map measured on the map.
3. the time I took for the walk.

I believe the figure stated for each walk to be very accurate but we all walk differently and not always in a straight line! The time allowed for each walk is on the generous side and does not include pub stops etc. The figure is based on the fact that on average a person walks 2 1/2 miles an hours but less in hilly terrain.

# REMEMBER AND OBSERVE THE COUNTRY CODE

 Enjoy the countryside and respect its life and work.

 Guard against all risk of fire.

 Fasten all gates.

 Keep your dogs under close control.

 Keep to public paths across farmland.

 Use gates and stiles to cross fences, hedges and walls.

 Leave livestock, crops and machinery alone.

 Take your litter home - pack it in; pack it out.

 Help to keep all water clean.

 Protect wildlife, plants and trees.

 Take special care on country roads

Make no unnecessary noise.

# THE HIKER'S CODE

❀  *Hike only along marked routes - do not leave the trail.*

❀  *Use stiles to climb fences; close gates.*

❀  *Camp only in designated campsites.*

❀  *Carry a light-weight stove.*

❀  *Leave the trail cleaner than you found it.*

❀  *Leave flowers and plants for others to enjoy.*

❀  *Keep dogs on a leash.*

❀  *Protect and do not disturb wildlife.*

❀  *Use the trail at your own risk.*

❀  *Leave only your thanks and footprints - take nothing but photographs.*

# EQUIPMENT NOTES
## ... some personal thoughts

**BOOTS** - *preferably with a full leather upper, of medium weight, with a vibram sole. I always add a foam cushioned insole to help cushion the base of my feet.*

**SOCKS** - *I generally wear two thick pairs as this helps minimise blisters. The inner pair are of loop stitch variety and approximately 80% wool. The outer are a thick rib pair of approximately 80% wool.*

**WATERPROOFS** - *for general walking I wear a T shirt or cotton shirt with a cotton wind jacket on top. You generate heat as you walk and I prefer to layer my clothes to avoid getting too hot. Depending on the season will dictate how many layers you wear. In soft rain I just use my wind jacket for I know it quickly dries out. In heavy or consistant rain I slip on a neoprene lined cagoule, and although hot and clammy it does keep me reasonably dry. Only in extreme conditions will I don overtrousers, much preferring to get wet and feel comfortable. I never wear gaiters!*

**FOOD** - *as I walk I carry bars of chocolate, for they provide instant energy and are light to carry. In winter a flask of hot coffee is welcome. I never carry water and find no hardship from not doing so, but this is a personal matter! From experience I find the more I drink the more I want and sweat. You should always carry some extra food such as trail mix & candy bars etc., for emergencies.*

**RUCKSACKS** - *for day walking I use a climbing rucksack of about 40 litre capacity and although it leaves excess space it does mean that the sac is well padded, with an internal frame and padded shoulder straps. Inside apart from the basics for one day I carry gloves, balaclava, spare pullover and a pair of socks.*

**MAP & COMPASS** - *when I am walking I always have the relevant map - preferably 1:25,000 scale - open in my hand. This enables me to constantly check that I am walking the right way. In case of bad weather I carry a compass, which once mastered gives you complete confidence in thick cloud or mist.*

SHORT CIRCULAR
WALKS
IN THE
DUKERIES

CRESWELL CRAGS          J.J. CREBER

by
JOHN N. MERRILL

Other
Nottinghamshire
Walk guides
by
John Merrill

SHORT CIRCULAR
WALKS IN SOUTH
NOTTINGHAMSHIRE

BY
JOHN N. MERRILL

# THE
# LITTLE JOHN
# CHALLENGE WALK

Fancy a challenge?
Try John Merrill's
**"Little John
Challenge Walk."**
- 28 miles around
Sherwood Forest
from Edwinstowe.
Badge and certificate
available on completion!
*Happy walking!*

## BY
## JOHN N. MERI

**THE LITTLE JOHN CHALLENGE WALK
by JOHN N. MERRILL**

John Merrill, the world's greatest walker, describes his
favourite 28 mile circular walk from Edwinstowe; the
heart of Robin Hood country and Sherwood Forest. The
walk is a challenge to complete in about ten hours, but
is well within the capabilities of the average person. The
walk encompasses the scenic character of the forest
with unspoilt villages, meandering rivers, gorges, and
historic houses. For those who complete the circuit a
special four colour embroidered badge and completion
certificate is available.

a J.N.M. PUBLICATION

£2.25

*"from footprint
to finished book"*

## CIRCULAR WALK GUIDES -

*SHORT CIRCULAR WALKS IN THE PEAK DISTRICT - Vol. 1 and 2*
*CIRCULAR WALKS IN WESTERN PEAKLAND*
*SHORT CIRCULAR WALKS IN THE STAFFORDSHIRE MOORLANDS*
*SHORT CIRCULAR WALKS - TOWNS & VILLAGES OF THE PEAK DISTRICT*
*SHORT CIRCULAR WALKS AROUND MATLOCK*
*SHORT CIRCULAR WALKS IN THE DUKERIES*
*SHORT CIRCULAR WALKS IN SOUTH YORKSHIRE*
*SHORT CIRCULAR WALKS IN SOUTH DERBYSHIRE*
*SHORT CIRCULAR WALKS AROUND BUXTON*
*SHORT CIRCULAR WALKS AROUND WIRKSWORTH*
*SHORT CIRCULAR WALKS IN THE HOPE VALLEY*
*40 SHORT CIRCULAR WALKS IN THE PEAK DISTRICT*
*CIRCULAR WALKS ON KINDER & BLEAKLOW*
*SHORT CIRCULAR WALKS IN SOUTH NOTTINGHAMSHIRE*
*SHIRT CIRCULAR WALKS IN CHESHIRE*
*SHORT CIRCULAR WALKS IN WEST YORKSHIRE*
*CIRCULAR WALKS TO PEAK DISTRICT AIRCRAFT WRECKS by John Mason*
*CIRCULAR WALKS IN THE DERBYSHIRE DALES*
*SHORT CIRCULAR WALKS IN EAST DEVON*
*SHORT CIRCULAR WALKS AROUND HARROGATE*
*SHORT CIRCULAR WALKS IN CHARNWOOD FOREST*
*SHORT CIRCULAR WALKS AROUND CHESTERFIELD*
*SHORT CIRCULAR WALKS IN THE YORKS DALES - Vol 1 - Southern area.*
*SHORT CIRCULAR WALKS IN THE AMBER VALLEY (Derbyshire)*
*SHORT CIRCULAR WALKS IN THE LAKE DISTRICT*
*SHORT CIRCULAR WALKS IN THE NORTH YORKSHIRE MOORS*
*SHORT CIRCULAR WALKS IN EAST STAFFORDSHIRE*
*DRIVING TO WALK - 16 Short Circular walks south of London by Dr. Simon Archer*
*LONG CIRCULAR WALKS IN THE PEAK DISTRICT - Vol.1 and 2.*
*LONG CIRCULAR WALKS IN THE STAFFORDSHIRE MOORLANDS*
*LONG CIRCULAR WALKS IN CHESHIRE*
*WALKING THE TISSINGTON TRAIL*
*WALKING THE HIGH PEAK TRAIL*
*WALKING THE MONSAL TRAIL & OTHER DERBYSHIRE TRAILS*

## CANAL WALKS -

*VOL 1 - DERBYSHIRE & NOTTINGHAMSHIRE*
*VOL 2 - CHESHIRE & STAFFORDSHIRE*
*VOL 3 - STAFFORDSHIRE*
*VOL 4 - THE CHESHIRE RING*
*VOL 5 - LINCOLNSHIRE & NOTTINGHAMSHIRE*
*VOL 6 - SOUTH YORKSHIRE*
*VOL 7 - THE TRENT & MERSEY CANAL*

## JOHN MERRILL DAY CHALLENGE WALKS -

*WHITE PEAK CHALLENGE WALK*
*DARK PEAK CHALLENGE WALK*
*PEAK DISTRICT END TO END WALKS*
*STAFFORDSHIRE MOORLANDS CHALLENGE WALK*
*THE LITTLE JOHN CHALLENGE WALK*